Bevel

WILLIAM LETFORD has worked as a roofer, on and off, since he was fifteen years old. He has received a New Writer's Award from the Scottish Book Trust and an Edwin Morgan Travel Bursary which allowed him to spend three months in the mountains of northern Italy helping to restore a medieval village. He has an M.Litt in Creative Writing from the University of Glasgow.

WILLIAM LETFORD

Bevel

CARCANET

First published in Great Britain in 2012 by

Carcanet Press Limited
Alliance House
Cross Street
Manchester M2 7AQ

www.carcanet.co.uk

A CIP catalogue record for this book is available from the British Library

ISBN 978 1 84777 192 6

The publisher acknowledges financial assistance from Arts Council England

Typeset by XL Publishing Services. Tiverton
Printed and bound in England by SRP Ltd, Exeter

for my mother, my father, and my sister

Acknowledgements

Some of these poems were first published in *New Poetries V* (Carcanet 2012), *i chose to listen* (Reel Festivals 2011), *New Writing from Scotland* (Scottish Book Trust 2009), *Mayfly* and *Poetry Scotland*.

Many thanks to Linda Jackson, Chris Powici, Magi Gibson, Ian Mcpherson, Alan Bisset, Ryan Van Winkle, the Stirling Writers' Group, the Arts Trust of Scotland and the Scotttish Book Trust for all their support over the years.

Contents

Waking for work in the winter

Even when frost hasn't left the hard ground rutted by the wheels of tractors
Even though tail-lights clog the motorway
Even though the moon still stands blind and cold in the morning sky
Even though the sheets are clean and the covers are warm
and the person beside you breathes the rise and fall of somewhere deep
Get up
Like the dog that hears a sound in the dark
Get up

Becoming

After work my grandfather would wash his hands in the kitchen sink
He would use Fairy Liquid as lather, and as a boy I'd watch him scrub stains
from his skin, clear dirt from his fingernails. Where have these hands been
I'd wonder, what is out there? Now, after each working each day I stare
at my own hands in my own sink. It's a powerful sensation. This mixture
of pride and sadness.

For the journey

When they told him who was beneath the boulder, he didn't say a word
just placed his forehead against it, then one hand, then two
then set his shoulder to work. None of the men had seen someone so
desperate, so methodical. The lamps on their helmets brightened his back
that shifted and bucked but wouldn't buckle. They watched as his boots
dug troughs in the dirt. Whenever he tired there'd be silence
then three deep breaths and he would go again. We should stop him
said one man. Leave him, said another, or he'll never know he couldn't lift it.

It's aboot the labour

hammers	nails
hammers	nails
hammers	nails

heh Casey did a tell ye a goat
a couple a poems published
widizthatmean
widayyemean
dizthatmeanyegetmoneyfurrit

eh	naw
aw	right

hammers	nails
hammers	nails
hammers	nails

Be prepared

wear three T-shirts and one hooded top
layers are important
they can always come off
remember your oilskins
it's always raining somewhere
wear a scarf
cold air moves down from the neck
wear gloves
they're useless when wet
but handy if you hit the wrong nail
pay attention to the moment
the way water drips
the way a spider scuttles
have a healthy fear of heights
when working from a ladder
know which way to fall
railings and slabs are unforgiving
flower beds and fuchsia bushes are better
practise your scream
if you strike your thumb with the hammer
don't squeal
roar like a lion
when the pain subsides and you look around
you'll know exactly what I mean
acknowledge the moon
it was part of the earth once
its loneliness can make you feel beautiful
lift properly
you'll need your back to make your money

coffee shop window

only children brave enough

to return my stare

Wit is it

The stonemason sade it's aw in yur heed
Yur eyes ur like windeez an yur brain's gon naywhere
Build yurself a palace

The plumber told mi no eh complicate things
Ivrythin's movin in one direction
We jist caerry it fur a while then lit it go

A sparky fay Partick sade it's impossible ti see
bit yu'll know when yuv found it
It'll stope yur hert deed an throw yi right oot yur boots

The labourer stood up, it's aboot strength, son
Wit kin yi caerry, wit kin yi leave behind

Roughcast Johnny sade it's three parts sand
an one part cement. It's aw in the mix

The joiner stubbed oot eez fag
If a man's goat the misyur eh eezsel
wit diz it mettur

A looked it the gaffer. Work hard, he sade
bit that wiz his answer fur ivrythin

Slate Knife Mcallum shouted fae the roof
It's aboot perspective, son, where eh yi standin
Wit eh yi lookin it

Then the rain came, heavy, bouncin
Pock marks appeared in Johnny's cement
Puddles wur jumpin aroond the sparky's feet

Half Brick Mcpherson pulled oan eez waterproofs
listen tae that, he sade, this is it, a think this is it

By the time we met

Candlelight was kind to her. Her fork seemed
weightless, but seldom made the journey upwards
I suspect that she had tasted asparagus before
Conversations clashed around her and dispersed
like circles on the surface of a lake
After the Shiraz, I had courage, and I said, *You
must have been something when you were younger*
Quiet, so none could overhear, she touched
my arm and replied, 'We stumble into youth
by accident, from somewhere else, and spend
the rest of our lives making our way home.'

We are

inside the kick
and crunch of colour
where autumn's taken its
dagger and opened up a vein

so the pavements aren't so grey
our heartbeats are not so
bleak and this kiss holds
more than warmth
and blood

Elderly ladies and afternoon tea

Plain and smooth and white
she tested the tablecloth
between thumb and finger

New   she asked

New   she replied

Then drew the flat of her hand
across the arm of her chair
to feel the fibres rise against her

Always loved this sofa   she said

Yes   she replied

Then unconsciously brushed
the lattice of veins
beneath the scarf around her neck

This spring evening

My window is open this spring evening. There is street noise
and summer is only one month away. Two hours ago my sister
placed the scan of her unborn baby on my kitchen table
embraced me to tell me she was pregnant, then left for work
River, she said, if it's a girl. So maybe I can see an arm. Maybe
I can see a leg. Either way, we are becoming acquainted
Tonight the instruments are beyond me. The music is constant

Fusion expands

Before Mercury melts and Venus has vanished
Before temperatures rise and our oceans boil
Before the ghost of our sun is outward bound
There will be one   last   perfect day

Worker

sweat the felt screed the cement
pack the joist level the cleat
eat the piece hammer the nail
                    string-line the future
                    raise the bones
                    build the skeletons
                    whistle the windows
                    into our rooms
                    hoist your brushes
                    sweep the sky

A bassline

Courses like a neutron star counting the immeasurable

Asteroids circle   Comets are everywhere   Then the funk

Comes back from oblivion and the mass begins to heave

A blonde-haired angel trapped in a pair of red hotpants

Turns to give me a grin so wide

I know it's not for me   It's for the whole fucking world

Newsflash

av hud enough
am kickin it in
am packin it up
am maikin a stand
am plantn ma flag
youz kin aw jist go tae fuck

cause thurs too many people
wae too many taunts
who know where thur gon
niver gettin wit they want

baws tae bein neck deep
bangin ma heed off a brick waw

Naw

am puntin masel up
it's time tae ascend
it's time tae evolve
am gonnae be immortal
like the stars in the sky
watchin this wee world revolve

inside ootside upside doonside backside frontside
al be the man
an then some mair

when a knoack oan death's door
he's gonnae be feart tae come oot
top eh the food chain?
tell him his fuckin tea's out

Hollow words in the black dog days

Sophie has a colleague at work, whose heart hasn't been broken
a virgin, she says, in the truest sense. Stephanie has a gym partner
with a walk that'll pull you in its wake, and Amanda has a hairdresser
whose brown eyes can drown out words. Spoilt for choice, they say
Bullshit, he replies. He tells them, that the leads in the old movies
have faded. That the beauties of antiquity are buried beneath the years
He tells them that everyone alive belongs to one season. He tells them
that the seasons move quickly.

Moths

Moths

Moths

Moths

fucking moths
perforated my kilt between weddings
larvae   somewhere in the bedroom
wardrobe   under the bed   i don't know   Moths
heads full of light bulbs   and moons   erratic
fucking moths   Moths

Moths

Moths

Moths

27

Taking a headbutt

your pal ruffled ma hat
i said, what? made the mistake of leaning forward
and that was that

blood-metal darkness and the taste of brass
the bell was rung
i know i went somewhere
because i had to come back

Working away

Mornings are familiar. The heft of a still-saw. The weight of a drill. The texture
of rust. When to say yes, when to say lift it yourself. But the evenings are foreign
The café in the piazza catches the sun at six. The waiter is openly bored. Workmen
drink wine, talk quietly, leave dust on the seats. Only the flies are busy. Yesterday
the grocer gave me tomatoes for free. Most of them were half rotten
So she used her thumb to show me where to cut.

In the mountains of northern Italy

The chapel on the hill has no roof. For five hundred years its four walls
have framed the universe. The locals laugh at the Sistine Chapel
and call it the coffin lid.

No holding back

Jesus Christ
Ten days in and kicked in the teeth
Scraping myself off the flowers

My god
The way she formed the English language
And how I enjoyed listening to it

Lord
Take back her nakedness
Wash the laughter away

Cleanse me
Of the dance in the abandoned church
Of the movement

Cure me

Or leave me with everything
The emptiness most of all
Let nothing fall away

Burn me
With memory

Breakfast in Baiardo

the window to my right is open
and filled with mountains
that layer the distance until
there is almost no room for sky

the key hung by the door
has been stretched tight by gravity
pulled into place
every chair in the room is empty

the sugar bag crackles
and a line along the cooker tells me
that the ants   are on the march

No distractions

A DONKEY BRAYING FURTHER DOWN THE HILL

What am i looking for? Why am i here?
Ten minutes spent watching the old woman
               feed
                        her
                             chickens
Smelling the shit, possibly her own
that she's thrown over the garden

Searching for something more

But sometimes shit is shit
And that's it. Full Stop
Cluck Cluck
am bored oot ma nut

A DONKEY BRAYING FURTHER DOWN THE HILL

The man that sits by the café everyday
Will be ninety-nine next month
if you ask him how he is
he will tell you
he is old

it rains
it rains
it rains

and the crickets

talk amongst themselves

Outside the city

lie down
on a cloudless night
look up

every star
visible to the eye
touches the ground

not strong enough
to reflect
but it's there

the grass is full of it
trees are alive with it

Sunburst

one astronomical unit eight light minutes ninety-three million miles
and right here bare chest top off beneath the sun god Ra
sweat beads arms ache heart pounding blue sky aware of my youth
aware of my strength above the noise of the street
a ridge to bed – a tile to repair – and the heat
one astronomical unit eight light minutes ninety-three million miles
and right here

T-shirt   wrapped   around my head   draped   over my shoulders

fierce heat   my shadow   like a pharaoh   god of the wall   bolster

hammer   chipping cement   taking it back   to the shape

of each stone   and the craft   of the hand   that placed it   his hand

my hand   same sun   same wall   dirt beneath me   alive

digger wasps   lifting dust   by the beat   and beat   of wings

today   three eggs   white   inside the wall   and a scorpion

inside the wall   HAMMER RAISED   its beating heart   stops me

digger wasps   the scorpion's heart   the beat   of my heart

the noise   of the hammer   the noise   of the bolster

pharaoh   where life   is free   there make me immortal

The light and dark of Adeona

People have come and gone but mostly
it's been me and her, sharing the kitchen
sharing the bathroom, sleeping on pallets
that lie four feet apart. It's quiet
so small things change the balance of a room
cutlery into the sink, the scrape of a chair
or the relentless persistence of Lilo and Stitch
played over again on a portable DVD player
She is nineteen, American, young for her age
Thinks it's more important to talk than have
something to say. This frustrates me, but we
get by fine. Except Wednesday last week
We'd caught the bus to town and returned
with more wine than usual. During the night
she pulled back my sheet. I said no
Later, l heard her on the terrace, crying
for father, asking the dark sky why her mother
wouldn't love her. At breakfast, her arms and legs
were crossed with shallow cuts. I asked
if she had fallen, this gave her the chance
to say yes. So I watch her more closely. Not out of
worry, or pity, out of interest. She is a person
of course, but she is also a story. Like now
out on the terrace again with a candle
set in front of her, no crying this time
because there are stars, and the sky is not dark.

A bad day

For thousands of years the great civilisations
considered manual and mundane labour
a punishment.
Then they abolished slavery
and began the slow process of brainwashing the minions.

Orchards

The train is moving
from Fiorenzuola to Parma
We're hot. It's Italy
We're supposed to be hot

Fiona takes
a set of four seats to herself
She reaches up
and snaps the window open
It's okay. She's pissed off
But not because it's hot

On the far side
of the River Arda
Fiona looks over and I feel
the rhythm of the train

It's not forever
that makes life beautiful

Helsinki, Finland

I go to their flat and it's cluttered with books and bookcases lean into rooms and they have a dog called Banton some type of cross that looks beautiful   knows it   chews books when-ever they're out cause it loves the taste of words and he is Kari Karlsson and she is Stella Karlsson and we eat rice biscuits with scrambled egg and butter then spinach pie with beer to chase it down and wine and cream sherry then cider with amaretto coffee afterward on the bus it's eleven o'clock and the young team are heading into town and I think I might just keep going past my stop get off and see what happens cause when you're away even the mundane is novel

Mhari and Annika

A lot of people listening it

Have these stripes that belong to different parts of the country then we have
two days dancing festivals and some traditional festivals and probably since I was five
I have gone

My mother was a dancer it was great

It's probably awful ya

Annika's English is awful

But it's poem

He's going to make a poem out of it?
How Finnish and Estonian are speaking English? oh my god
I had so much wine

Our life

Love it, she says
like you can't have it and never will, like it's someone else's
then love me like that, as if I don't love you. As if I might
at any moment, walk away, and don't just love me, hate me
because that's important too. Hate the way I make you feel
and never let that go. Love me, she says
like I love you

Café culture

Wur hivin a pint
oan a table ootside
cause it's a nice day
an he says

A love the summer
it's hoat
ye kin wear yer shoarts
the burds –
trouble is bit
ivery time a go oot fur a powercaird
a end up pished

Don't you think i know

the roots
must've driven deep
to draw life
from the mantle
jacked
into the bubbling engine
of molten rock
its branches
leap from the trunk
and give birth
to leaves
that flicker like sparks
encased in green

i want to look away
but i can't
and she's
standing in front of me
lashing me with her tears
and the same two questions

where were you
what were you thinking
where were you
what were you thinking

Let's just be

Aye   Okay
keep in touch
every week or two
every month

Good idea

let's be
limbo acquaintances
let's think about
what we've lost
wander around
inside the ghost
of our relationship

Naw

How about

Better nothing said
how about
better alive and severed
than connected
half-dead

Sex poem number 1

aye   right   okay   right right   okay

Prowl: Sex poem number 2

should've called it a night after the second drink
but the primal inside me had to follow it through
to sex – and that was just noises in the dark
two people rooting around for something beautiful
so we could grind it
to dust

Sex poem number 3

buckles belts buttons clips
jeans jeans
socks
stretch for the socks
negotiate the heel
negotiate the heel
pants
slow for the pants
then another person's skin
fingertips fine hairs follicles
then couch to carpet
elbows knees
focus
acknowledge the clues
quickness of breath
pressure on shoulders
pressure on hips
don't get distant
smile
make eye contact
love
if at all possible
love

Impact theory

It is 4.13am on New Year's Day 2010. My curtains are half closed. Moonlight shows me the girl sleeping with her back toward me. She has the outlines of stars tattooed onto her spine. Each one smaller until the void beneath the duvet makes it difficult to see. Tonight is the first time we've met. With the tips of my fingers I touch the distance between the first two stars. Then I half that distance, and half it again, and half it again. Because infinity isn't space and time, it's a process.

Thurs hunnurs a burds oan the roofs

here huw chouf wouf wee robin rid tit peejin breesty lovey dovey
ruffle yur feathers show me yur plume look it that Frank nut a look
nut a nut plod on then mouldy breed heed woop woop look it that
fingle foogle boogaloo that's no even a crow that's a dinosaur
thur'll be teeth in that beak that's fur sure ohh beady eye beady eye
get behind the gable she's fae the social wit a life Frank wit a life
feedin oan scraps huntin fur crumbs bit listen tae this listen tae this
we're no dodos we kin fly forget aboot the fields Frank look it the sky

They speak of the gods

He says Hades, and I see Richard, wearing his welding mask
kneeling beside a stripped out Citroën, sparks from his torch
lighting one side of the garage wall. She says Zeus, and I see
Casey, framed against the sky, bloated and happy
carrying cement across a tiled roof.

For the spirit

Often, over dinner, or during parties, or post-reading, someone will say
winter on the roofs must be hard. I'll reply, yes, then discuss cracked lips
cold slates, wet gloves. But really, summer is too easy. It's all about t-shirts
and sunlight in the room before you wake up. In winter I fight fifteen battles
from my duvet to the front door, and win. So keep your tanned skin
give me frost on the fence wire, and January.

Chimneys

sunshine   workmen
work on slate roofs

above half-shadowed
streets   hammers

echo against shale
dropped

from scaffold
to skip   casting clouds

that billow beneath
pigeons   that sweep

like the sparkle
of light against water

The songs we love

I don't know how many people she'd slept with
it's not often that you do. I had an idea she'd
travelled with bands. Bands that had made it big
I'm talking stadiums, television adverts, songs
that could penetrate your day while you're buying
boxer shorts. But I liked that, her history was present
She'd smile sometimes when one of my friends
mentioned this concert, or that concert, and I'd get
jealous. I would imagine groupies. Bodies on beds
King size mattresses that couldn't contain the sex
Her tattoos were names of men. 'Foreign rivers'
she'd say. But you know, I had the feeling she'd lived
I liked that too. She reminded me of vinyl, and she
loved vinyl. She'd often sit cross legged
and drunk in front of her record player. Playing
record after record. Listening intently
to the versions of herself still alive inside the music.

Schrödinger

perhaps we would be
both dead and alive
unless the box was open
and someone was watching

Sunday, with the television off

I think of the future. My death bed. I imagine the man I will be. Then I pay that man a visit. Ask him, what would you do?

So I leave the car and walk across town. Knock on my fathers' door to say hello and listen to his stories, the ones I've heard before.

It's like I've travelled in time. Now he knows that someone is listening. On the way home, the sun falls behind the buildings, and I walk into a supermarket.

Winter in the world

The old lady struggles, footsteps careful, leaving shuffle marks in the snow
No shopping bag, so maybe it's church, and maybe not. Perhaps she is out
for a walk, because she can, and the night is spare, and she is undiminished
and harder than bone.

A poem

Is an object made of language

A poem
Should pass from fire to fire – from chest to chest

A poem
Does not belong to the poet